My First Pet Library **from the** American Humane Association

My First Dog

American Humane®

Protecting
Children & Animals
Since 1877

Enslow Elementary
an imprint of
Enslow Publishers, Inc.
40 Industrial Road
Box 398
Berkeley Heights, NJ 07922
USA

http://www.enslow.com

Linda Bozzo

American Humane ®

Protecting
Children & Animals
Since 1877

Founded in 1877, the American Humane Association is the oldest national organization dedicated to protecting both children and animals. Through a network of child and animal protection agencies and individuals, the American Humane Association develops policies, legislation, curricula, and training programs to protect children and animals from abuse, neglect, and exploitation. To learn how you can support the vision of a nation where no child or animal will ever be a victim of willful abuse or neglect, visit www.americanhumane.org, phone (303) 792-9900, or write to the American Humane Association at 63 Inverness Drive East, Englewood, Colorado, 80112-5117.

● ●

This book is dedicated to my husband and daughters, who never stop believing in me, and to pet lovers everywhere.

The editor wishes to dedicate this book to her very first dog, Frank N. Furter, the bravest dachshund of all.

● ●

Library of Congress Cataloging-in-Publication Data

Bozzo, Linda.
  My first dog / Linda Bozzo.
    p. cm. — (My first pet library from the American Humane Association)
    Includes bibliographical references and index.
  ISBN 13: 978-0-7660-2754-1
  ISBN 10: 0-7660-2754-6
    1. Dogs—Juvenile literature. I. Title.
  II. Series: Bozzo, Linda. My first pet library from the American Humane Association.
  SF427.B69 2007
  636.7—dc22
                                    2006008404

Printed in the United States of America

10 9 8 7 6 5 4 3 2

To Our Readers: We have done our best to make sure all Internet Addresses in this book were active and appropriate when we went to press. However, the author and the publisher have no control over and assume no liability for the material available on those Internet sites or on other Web sites they may link to. Any comments or suggestions can be sent by e-mail to comments@enslow.com or to the address on the back cover.

Every effort has been made to locate all copyright holders of material used in this book. If any errors or omissions have occurred, corrections will be made in future editions of this book.

Illustration Credits: Brand X Pictures, pp. 3, 4, 10, 21, 31; Comstock Images, pp. 6, 7, 11 (top), 16, 17; Eyewire, pp. 15, 26, 27; image100, pp. 19, 20; © 2006 Jupiterimages, pp. 5, 8, 11 (bottom), 13 (tag) 14, 22, 23; Painetworks, pp. 9, 25, 28; Shutterstock, pp. 1, 13; Courtesy of Beth Townsend, p. 12.

Cover Credits: Photodisc.

Contents

World Almanac 16.95 11/2007

Great Pals

There is nothing more exciting than having a dog as a pet. A dog can add fun and love to your family.

Whether they are playing or curling up with you, dogs make great pals. There are many different kinds of dogs. Finding the right one for you is important.

This book can help answer questions you may have about finding and caring for that special dog.

Dogs need your attention.

Dogs are cute and love to play.

What Kind of Dog Do I Want?

Talk to your family. You might want an older dog. You might want a puppy. Dogs come in many sizes. Pick the kind of dog that is best for your family.

Older dogs are not as playful, but need less training.

Puppies are small and cute,
but need a lot of training.

Where is the Best Place to Find a Dog?

A great place to find a dog is at an **animal shelter**. Some people **adopt** dogs from friends or neighbors. You can also adopt a dog from a rescue group. Rescue groups save animals and make sure they go to good homes.

There are many dogs at animal shelters that need families.

What Will My Dog Need?

A dog should have his own special place to sleep or rest. He will also need a place to eat. He should have a food dish and a water dish.

Always remember to feed your dog.

Your dog will need food and clean water. Will your dog spend a lot of time outside? She will also need a doghouse to protect her from the weather.

Your new dog will need a collar with a tag. The tag should have your:

- Dog's name
- Family's name
- Address
- Phone number

If he gets lost, the tag will help him get returned safely.

Ask your **vet**, or animal doctor, about putting a **microchip** under your dog's skin. If your dog gets lost and loses his collar and tag, the microchip can help find out who the owner is.

Do not forget a leash for walking your dog.

Like you, dogs need safe toys to play with. Dogs like balls, chew toys, and stuffed animals made just for them.

Remember
to use a
leash when
you walk
your dog.

How Will I Keep My Dog Clean?

You can give your dog a bath. Some dogs need baths more often than others.

Giving your dog a bath can be fun!

comb

Keep your dog groomed.

nail clippers

brush

slicker brush

Brush your dog's hair. You should keep her teeth and ears clean. It is important to trim her nails. A **groomed** dog is a happy dog.

Is My New Dog Healthy?

You will need to take her to the vet for checkups. The vet will check your dog's eyes, ears, and nose.

A dog needs shots to protect it from illness. These shots are called **vaccinations**.

A vet is an animal doctor.

Spaying and **neutering** are operations that dogs have so they cannot have unwanted puppies. Female dogs can be spayed. Male dogs can be neutered. These operations can also help dogs stay healthy. They can also help dogs become more friendly.

Your vet can answer any questions about your pet's care.

Ask a vet any questions about your dog's health.

Does My Dog Need Exercise?

Yes, just like you, dogs need exercise and fresh air to stay healthy. You can take your dog for walks. You can play ball with her in your yard.

Walking dogs can be fun for everyone.

Catch is a fun game to play with your dog.

Can I Leave My Dog Home Alone?

Yes, but he may need to be trained. He might bark a lot at first. He might even chew on things like your shoes! If this happens, do not worry. Your dog may just need to get used to his new home. Start by leaving him alone for only a few minutes at a time. Soon you will be able to leave him longer.

You may wish to make a special place or den for your dog. Your dog can go there to feel safe.

Like you, dogs can get sad and lonely if they are left alone.

A **crate** can be used as this special place. You can also use the crate to keep your dog in while you are away for short periods of time. This will help protect your belongings until he learns not to chew things.

You and Your Dog

Big, small, young, or old, all dogs need one thing—a good home. So, play with him. Love him. Keep him healthy and happy. You and your dog will be perfect pals for many years.

Treat your dog like part of the family.

Show your dog love and she will love you back.

Words to Know

adopt—To take into your family.

animal shelter—A place where animals that need homes are kept.

crate—An indoor doghouse.

groom—To clean and brush your dog.

microchip—A small computer chip. It can be put under a dog's skin. If your dog gets lost, the microchip can be scanned by a special computer. This will show who owns the dog.

neutering—An operation male dogs have so they cannot produce puppies.

slicker brush—A special brush that removes dirt and loose hair from a dog's coat.

spaying—An operation female dogs have so they cannot have puppies.

vaccinations—Shots that a dog needs to protect against illness.

vet—Vet is short for veterinarian, a doctor who takes care of animals.

Read About

BOOKS

Blackaby, Susan. *A Dog For You: Caring For Your Dog.* Minneapolis, Minn.: Picture Window Books, 2003.

Gutman, Bill. *Adopting Pets: How to Choose Your New Best Friend.* Brookfield, Conn.: Millbrook Press, 2001.

Lauber, Patricia. *The True-or-False Book of Dogs.* New York: HarperCollins, 2003.

Simon, Seymour. *Dogs.* New York: HarperCollins Publishers, 2004.

Sjonger, Rebecca, and Bobbie Kaman. *Puppies.* New York: Crabtree Pub. Co., 2004.

INTERNET ADDRESSES

American Humane Association
  <http://www.americanhumane.org>
  Learn more about animals at this Web site.

How to Love Your Dog: A Kid's Guide to Dog Care
  <http://www.loveyourdog.com>
  Get helpful hints about dogs and their care at this great site.

Index